Trendi Mindi

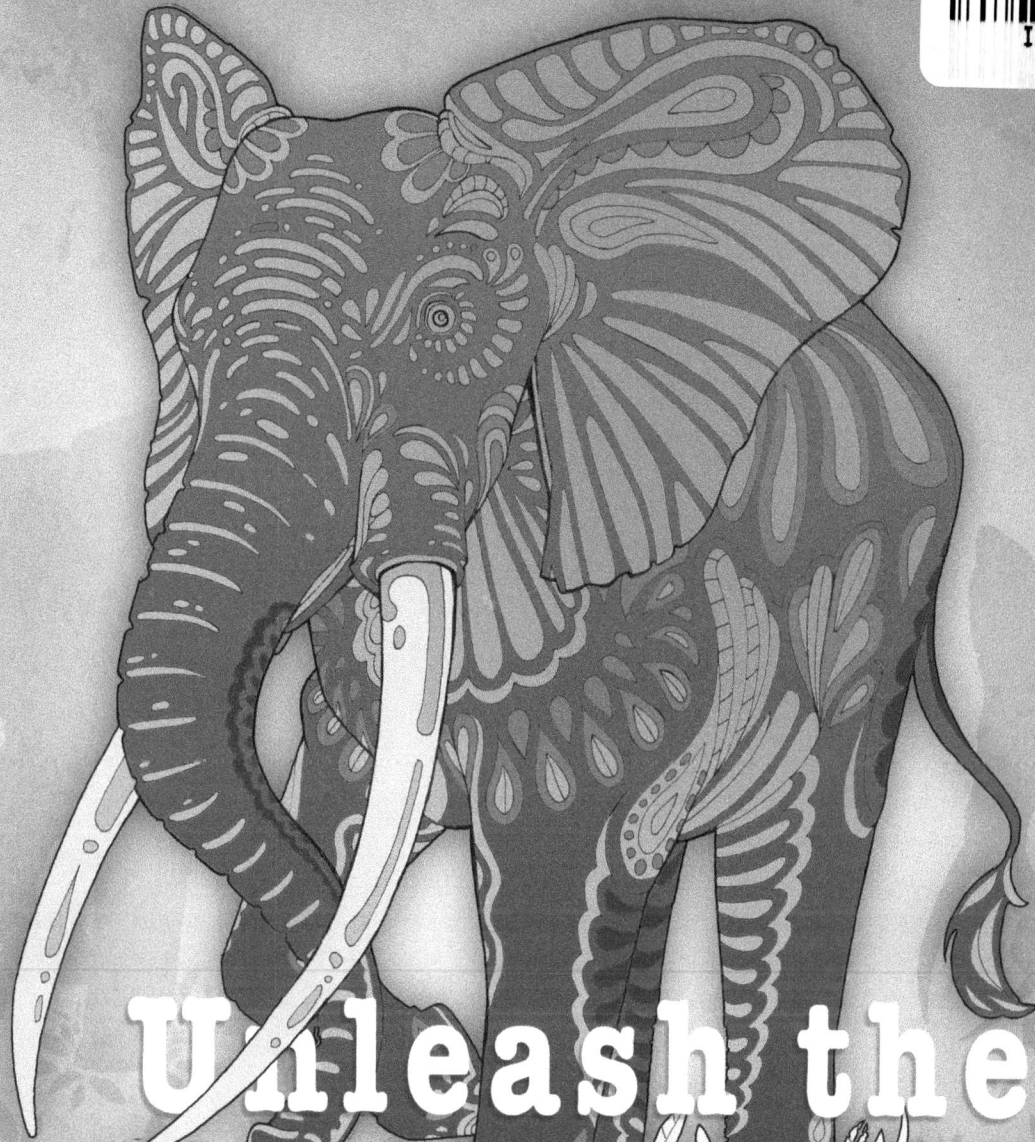

Unleash the
ANIMAL
Within
(the lines)

Adult Coloring Books: Best Sellers of Animals
(Dogs, Cats, Owls and More)

Come Join Me!

Stay updated on my new arrivals.

www.trendimindi.com

I am thrilled to see you have purchased my one of my many books! I hope you get as much enjoyment out of them as I do creating them. I can guarantee my books will bring you peace and tranquility. Sit back, relax, and let your inner artist run wild.

Happy Coloring!

Trendi Mindi

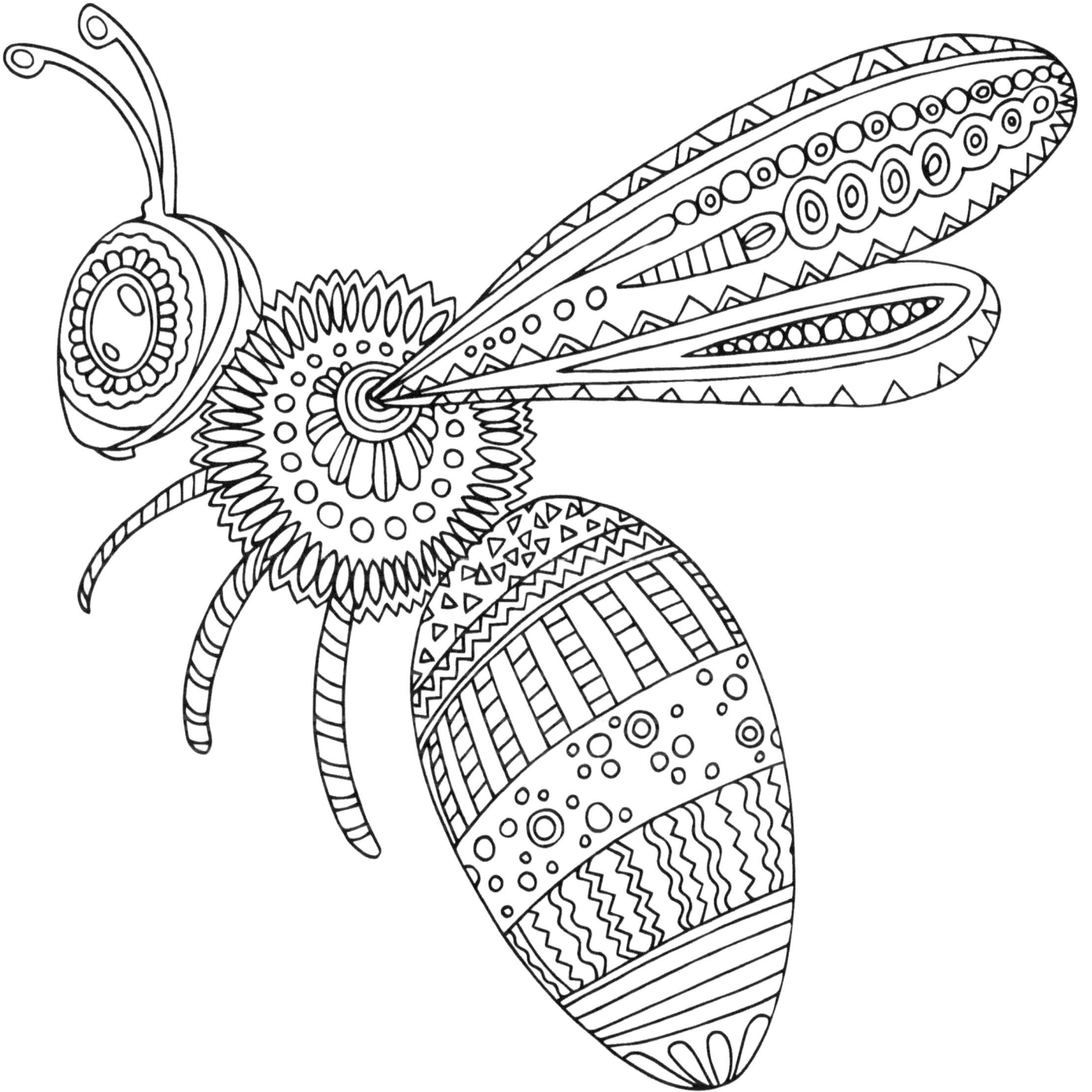

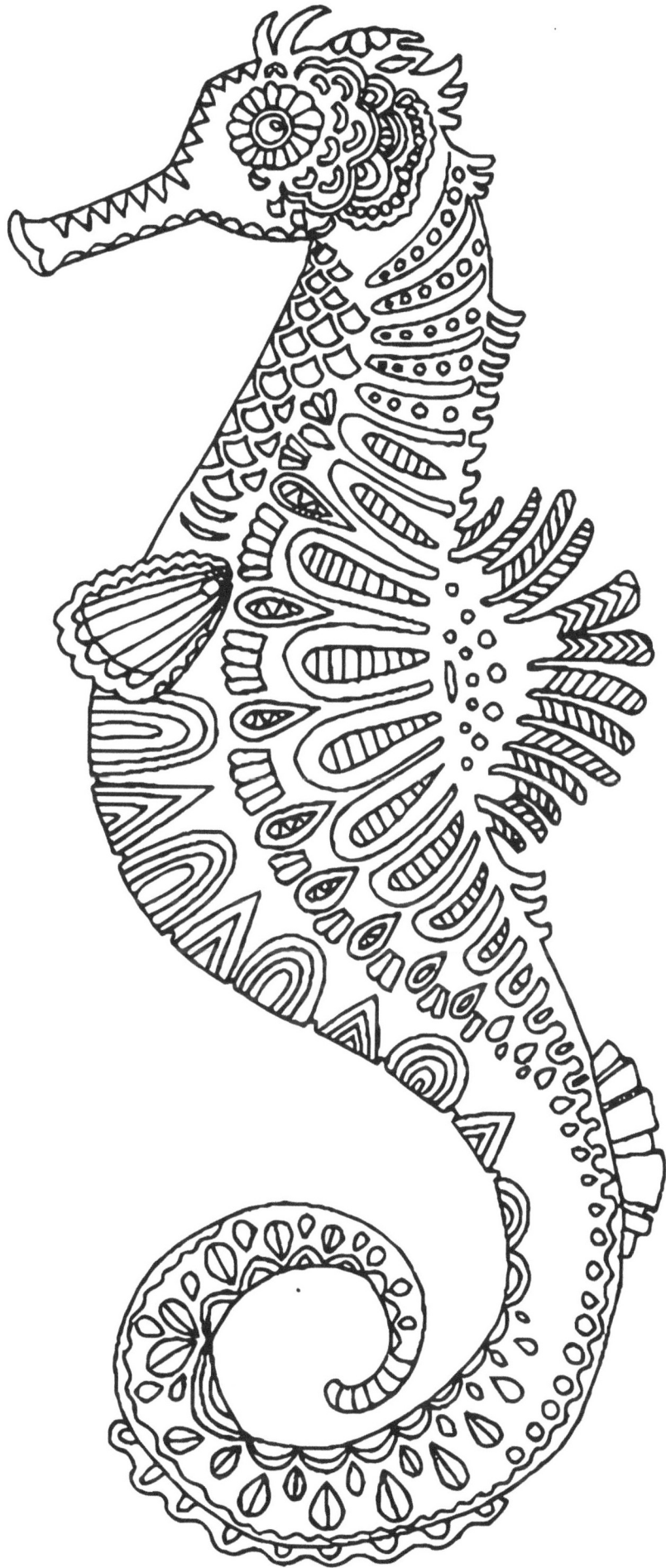